CONTENTS

Title	Page	CD Track
All Shook Up	2	1
Blue Suede Shoes	3	2
Can't Help Falling in Love	4	3
Don't Be Cruel (To a Heart That's True)	5	4
Hound Dog	6	5
I Want You, I Need You, I Love You	7	6
It's Now or Never	8	7
Jailhouse Rock	9	8
Love Me	10	9
Love Me Tender	11	10
Loving You	12	11
Return to Sender	13	12
(Let Me Be Your) Teddy Bear	14	13
Too Much	15	14
Wear My Ring Around Your Neck	16	15
B♭ Tuning Notes		16

HOW TO USE THE CD ACCOMPANIMENT:

THE CD IS PLAYABLE ON ANY CD PLAYER, AND IS ALSO ENHANCED SO MAC AND PC USERS CAN ADJUST THE RECORDING TO ANY TEMPO WITHOUT CHANGING THE PITCH.

A MELODY CUE APPEARS ON THE RIGHT CHANNEL ONLY. IF YOUR CD PLAYER HAS A BALANCE ADJUSTMENT, YOU CAN ADJUST THE VOLUME OF THE MELODY BY TURNING DOWN THE RIGHT CHANNEL.

Elvis and Elvis Presley are registered trademarks of Elvis Presley Enterprises, Inc.
Elvis image used by permission, © EPE

www.elvis.com

ISBN 978-1-4234-6670-3

HAL•LEONARD® CORPORATION
7777 W. BLUEMOUND RD. P.O. BOX 13819 MILWAUKEE, WI 53213

Visit Hal Leonard Online at
www.halleonard.com

◆ ALL SHOOK UP

FLUTE

Words and Music by OTIS BLACKWELL
and ELVIS PRESLEY

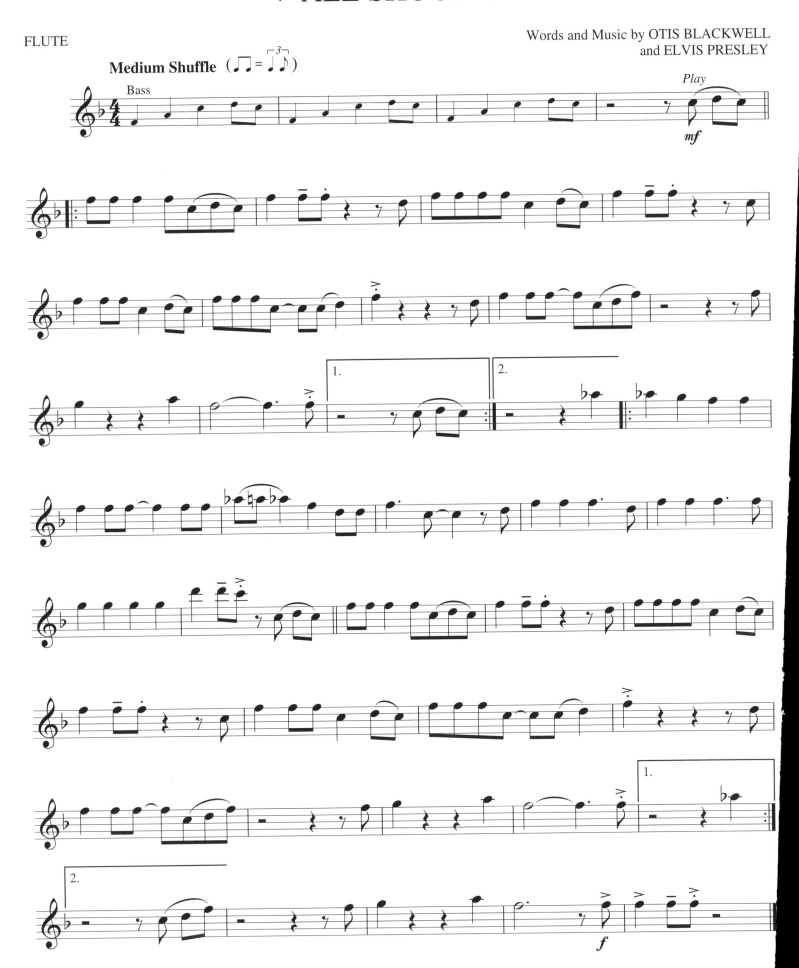

❷ BLUE SUEDE SHOES

Flute

Words and Music by
CARL LEE PERKINS

◆ CAN'T HELP FALLING IN LOVE

FLUTE

Words and Music by GEORGE DAVID WEISS,
HUGO PERETTI and LUIGI CREATORE

◆4 DON'T BE CRUEL
(To a Heart That's True)

Flute

Words and Music by OTIS BLACKWELL
and ELVIS PRESLEY

◆ HOUND DOG

FLUTE

Words and Music by JERRY LEIBER
and MIKE STOLLER

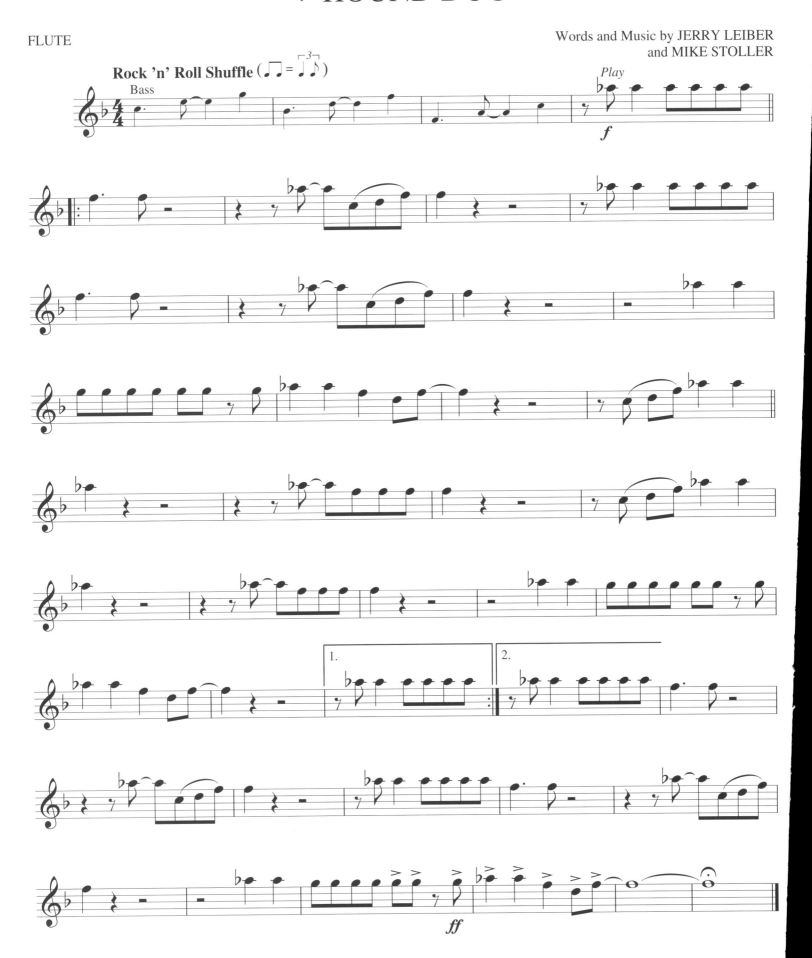

◆6 I WANT YOU, I NEED YOU, I LOVE YOU

FLUTE

Words and Music by MAURICE MYSELS
and IRA KOSLOFF

❼ IT'S NOW OR NEVER

Words and Music by AARON SCHROEDER
and WALLY GOLD

FLUTE

◆8 JAILHOUSE ROCK

Flute

Words and Music by JERRY LEIBER
and MIKE STOLLER

Rock 'n' Roll

◆9 LOVE ME

Flute

Words and Music by JERRY LEIBER
and MIKE STOLLER

LOVE ME TENDER

FLUTE

Words and Music by ELVIS PRESLEY
and VERA MATSON

Slowly, with feeling

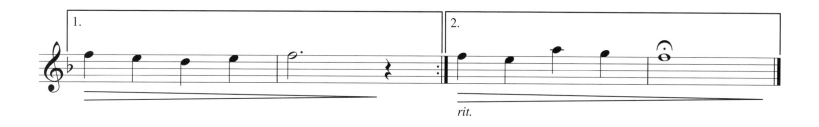

◆ 11 LOVING YOU

Flute

Words and Music by JERRY LEIBER
and MIKE STOLLER

RETURN TO SENDER

FLUTE

Words and Music by OTIS BLACKWELL
and WINFIELD SCOTT

◆13 (LET ME BE YOUR) TEDDY BEAR

FLUTE

Words and Music by KAL MANN
and BERNIE LOWE

◆14 TOO MUCH

Flute

Words and Music by LEE ROSENBERG
and BERNARD WEINMAN

WEAR MY RING AROUND YOUR NECK

Flute

Words and Music by BERT CARROLL
and RUSSELL MOODY